Sociology

Sociology

Issues and Debates

Edited by
Steve Taylor

MACMILLAN

First published 1999 by
MACMILLAN PRESS LTD
Houndmills, Basingstoke, Hampshire RG21 6XS
and London
Companies and representatives throughout the world

ISBN 0–333–67619–X hardcover
ISBN 0–333–67620–3 paperback

A catalogue record for this book is available
from the British Library.

This book is printed on paper suitable for recycling and
made from fully managed and sustained forest sources.

10 9   8   7   6 5   4   3   2   1
08 07 06 05 04 03 02 01 00 99

Editing and origination by
Aardvark Editorial, Mendham, Suffolk

Printed and bound in Great Britain by
Creative Print and Design (Wales), Ebbw Vale

Contents

Contents

nalytic categories to the study of non-western societies. She
g a book on the concept of culture.

s worked in sociology and political science departments in
at Britain and Australia. He is Professor of Political Science
hool of Social Sciences at the Australian National Univer-
He has published widely in the areas of social and political
ecent books are *Discourses of Power: From Hobbes to Foucault*
and *Governing Australia: Studies in Contemporary Rational-*
(edited with M. Dean, Cambridge University Press, 1998).
ok on democracy.

rofessor of Women's Studies and Director of the Centre for
t the University of York. She is the author of *Childhood and*
ell, 1982) and *Christine Delphy* (Sage, 1996). She has co-
udies: A Reader* (Harvester Wheatsheaf, 1993), *The Politics*
mption: Critical Readings* (Prentice Hall/Harvester Wheat-
Feminism and Sexuality* (Edinburgh University Press, 1996).
shed a number of articles on romance, sexuality and family
is currently researching the impact of risk and adult risk
veryday world of children. Forthcoming books include
sexuality* (Sage) and *Contemporary Feminist Theories* (Edin-
Press).

is Professor in the Department of Social Policy and the
n's Studies at the University of York. Her work focuses on
ender, 'race' and ethnicity, ageing, feminist and social theory
ocial research methodology. Her most recent book is *Science*
on of Women* (University College London Press, 1997). She
ok on feminist social research and initiating projects on
g.

Professor and Head of the Department of Sociology at the
sgow. He has written widely on the theory and history of
ational migration and on the history of capitalist develop-
publications include *Racism after 'Race Relations'* (Rout-
d (edited with D. Thranhardt) *Migration and European*
r, 1995).

is Senior Lecturer in Organizational Analysis at Warwick
the University of Warwick. Previously, he worked at
ness School. He has published a number of books and arti-
e of work and organizations, including *Organizations in*
an, 1990) and *Regulation and Deregulation in European*
(edited with D. Knights, Macmillan, 1997). His current
are primarily concerned with the impact of national and

List of Tables

List of Figures

Notes on

Robert Burgess is Vice-Chan
formerly Pro-Vice-Chancellor,
Sociology at the University of
research methodology and the
entitled *Beyond the First Degre*
Careers (1997).

Rosemary Crompton is Profes
She has previously taught at t
Anglia. She has researched wid
employment. Her most recent l
(Oxford University Press), *Clas*
turing Gender Relations and Emp

Grace Davie is Senior Lecturer
is author of *Religion in Britain S*
a book on religion in modern l
written numerous articles on th
she was General Secretary of
of Religion.

David Downes is Professor of
Mannheim Centre for Crimino
School of Economics. His book
Rock, 1966), *Understanding L*
Postwar Penal Policy in the Nether
Editor of the *British Journal of C*

Natalie Fenton is Lecturer in
Women's Studies in the Depar
University. Her books include
K. Richardson) and *Mediatin*
A. Bryman). Her current researc
voluntary sector and the media,
tion of public issues.

Christine Helliwell has taught
universities and is Senior Lecture
University in Canberra. She has
in New Zealand and Borneo. He
cultural theory. Many of her pub

applying western
is currently writin

Barry Hindess h
universities in Gre
in the Research S
sity in Canberra.
theory. His most
(Blackwell, 1996)
ities of Government
He is writing a be

Stevi Jackson is I
Women's Studies
Sexuality (Blackw
edited *Women's St*
of Domestic Consu
sheaf, 1995) and I
She has also publ
relationships and
anxiety on the e
Concerning Heter
burgh University

Mary Maynard
Centre for Wome
issues related to g
and feminist and s
and the Constructi
is finishing a bo
women and agein

Robert Miles is
University of Gla
racism, on intern
ment. His recent
ledge, 1993) an
Integration (Pinte

Glenn Morgan
Business School
Manchester Busi
cles in the sphe
Society (Macmill
Financial Services
research interests

List of Tables

List of Figures

Notes on Contributors

Robert Burgess is Vice-Chancellor of the University of Leicester and was formerly Pro-Vice-Chancellor, Director of CEDAR and Professor of Sociology at the University of Warwick. He has published widely on social research methodology and the sociology of education. His latest volume is entitled *Beyond the First Degree: Graduate Education, Lifelong Learning and Careers* (1997).

Rosemary Crompton is Professor of Sociology at City University, London. She has previously taught at the Universities of Leicester, Kent and East Anglia. She has researched widely in the sociology of work and women's employment. Her most recent books are *Women and Work in Modern Britain* (Oxford University Press), *Class and Stratification* (Polity Press) and *Restructuring Gender Relations and Employment* (Oxford University Press).

Grace Davie is Senior Lecturer in Sociology at the University of Exeter. She is author of *Religion in Britain Since 1945* (Blackwell, 1994) and is preparing a book on religion in modern Europe for Oxford University Press. She has written numerous articles on the sociology of religion. From 1994 to 1998 she was General Secretary of the International Society for the Study of Religion.

David Downes is Professor of Social Administration and Director of the Mannheim Centre for Criminology and Criminal Justice at the London School of Economics. His books include *The Delinquent Solution* (with Paul Rock, 1966), *Understanding Deviance* (1998) and *Contrasts in Tolerance: Postwar Penal Policy in the Netherlands and England and Wales* (1993). He was Editor of the *British Journal of Criminology* from 1985 to 1990.

Natalie Fenton is Lecturer in Communication and Media Studies and Women's Studies in the Department of Social Sciences at Loughborough University. Her books include *Nuclear Reactions* (with J. Corner and K. Richardson) and *Mediating Social Science* (with D. Deacon and A. Bryman). Her current research interests are the media and resistance, the voluntary sector and the media, alternative media and the popular presentation of public issues.

Christine Helliwell has taught both sociology and anthropology at several universities and is Senior Lecturer in Anthropology at the Australian National University in Canberra. She has carried out extensive ethnographic research in New Zealand and Borneo. Her primary research interests lie in social and cultural theory. Many of her publications are concerned with the difficulty of applying western analytic categories to the study of non-western societies. She is currently writing a book on the concept of culture.

Barry Hindess has worked in sociology and political science departments in universities in Great Britain and Australia. He is Professor of Political Science in the Research School of Social Sciences at the Australian National University in Canberra. He has published widely in the areas of social and political theory. His most recent books are *Discourses of Power: From Hobbes to Foucault* (Blackwell, 1996) and *Governing Australia: Studies in Contemporary Rationalities of Government* (edited with M. Dean, Cambridge University Press, 1998). He is writing a book on democracy.

Stevi Jackson is Professor of Women's Studies and Director of the Centre for Women's Studies at the University of York. She is the author of *Childhood and Sexuality* (Blackwell, 1982) and *Christine Delphy* (Sage, 1996). She has co-edited *Women's Studies: A Reader* (Harvester Wheatsheaf, 1993), *The Politics of Domestic Consumption: Critical Readings* (Prentice Hall/Harvester Wheatsheaf, 1995) and *Feminism and Sexuality* (Edinburgh University Press, 1996). She has also published a number of articles on romance, sexuality and family relationships and is currently researching the impact of risk and adult risk anxiety on the everyday world of children. Forthcoming books include *Concerning Heterosexuality* (Sage) and *Contemporary Feminist Theories* (Edinburgh University Press).

Mary Maynard is Professor in the Department of Social Policy and the Centre for Women's Studies at the University of York. Her work focuses on issues related to gender, 'race' and ethnicity, ageing, feminist and social theory and feminist and social research methodology. Her most recent book is *Science and the Construction of Women* (University College London Press, 1997). She is finishing a book on feminist social research and initiating projects on women and ageing.

Robert Miles is Professor and Head of the Department of Sociology at the University of Glasgow. He has written widely on the theory and history of racism, on international migration and on the history of capitalist development. His recent publications include *Racism after 'Race Relations'* (Routledge, 1993) and (edited with D. Thranhardt) *Migration and European Integration* (Pinter, 1995).

Glenn Morgan is Senior Lecturer in Organizational Analysis at Warwick Business School, the University of Warwick. Previously, he worked at Manchester Business School. He has published a number of books and articles in the sphere of work and organizations, including *Organizations in Society* (Macmillan, 1990) and *Regulation and Deregulation in European Financial Services* (edited with D. Knights, Macmillan, 1997). His current research interests are primarily concerned with the impact of national and